# PIZZAS AND MELTS

KÖNEMANN

# Party Pizzas

These delicious morsels are popular with all age groups and are ideal finger food for festive occasions. Fun to make and offering a range of tastes, these pizzas will give much enjoyment to your guests.

### Olive-Garlic Pitta Wedges

Remove most of the papery outside skin from 2 whole large heads of garlic; place in a baking pan and drizzle with olive oil. Bake in preheated moderate 180°C oven for 1 hour until soft. Remove from pan and cool. Squeeze softened flesh into a bowl and mash with a fork. Spread garlic paste onto 4 small pitta breads, top with 120 g pitted, chopped kalamata olives and 1 cup grated mozzarella cheese. Place on baking trays and cook for 15 minutes or until cheese is melted and golden. Cut each pitta into 6 small wedges and serve immediately. Makes 24.

### Prawn and Pesto Toasts

Cut a day-old bread stick into 1 cm slices, place on an oven tray in a single layer and bake in moderate 180°C oven for 10 minutes, turning once, until dry and crisp but not browned. When cool, spread slices with 3/4 cup pesto, and top with 350 g small school prawns (about 4 on each). Thinly slice 250 g bocconcini and lay over prawns. Place on oven trays and bake for 10 minutes or until cheese has melted. Note that bocconcini does not brown like other cheeses. Makes about 45.

### Smoked Salmon Triangles

Take 2 sheets of puff pastry and cut each into 9 squares, then each square in half diagonally to make 18 triangles. Place on greased oven trays and bake for 5 minutes at 180°C. Remove from oven and flatten slightly. Cut a 125 g round of brie into 36 thin wedges (the cheese is easy to cut when cold), and place one on each triangle. Top with slices of smoked salmon and bake a further 7 minutes or until pastry is lightly golden. Top with sprigs of dill. Serve immediately. Makes 36.

---

*Top three clockwise from left: Olive-Garlic Pitta Wedges, Prawn and Pesto Toasts and Smoked Salmon Triangles*

### Peperoni Rounds

Thinly slice 125 g peperoni and cook in a non-stick frypan until lightly golden; drain on paper towel. Cut 150 g cherry tomatoes into 4 slices each. Top round salted dry biscuits from a 250 g packet with peperoni, tomato and 100 g thinly sliced cheddar cheese. Cook under a hot grill until cheese is bubbling, serve immediately. Makes about 65.

### Bacon Pizza Bites

Finely chop 6 rashers bacon and cook in non-stick frying pan until golden brown; drain on paper towel. Divide $2/3$ cup pizza sauce between 4 small pizza bases (about 15 cm diameter) and spread evenly over surface. Sprinkle with cooked bacon and top with 1 cup finely grated mozzarella. Bake 15 minutes in moderate 180°C oven. Garnish with fresh chives. Cut each into 8 wedges and serve. Makes 32.

### Pissaladiere Squares

Finely slice 5 medium onions. Cook in tablespoon of oil over low heat for 20 minutes until very soft and lightly golden. Stir frequently to prevent sticking and burning; set aside to cool. Take 2 sheets of puff pastry and divide $1/3$ cup olive paste between each, spreading evenly over surface. Cut each sheet of pastry into 36 small squares. Place a small pile of onion mixture on each square. Cut 18 cherry tomatoes into quarters. Lay a piece on each square, topped by small pieces of anchovy. Place on greased oven trays; bake in preheated moderate 180°C oven for 15–20 minutes or until puffed and crisp. Serve. Makes 72.

### Ham & Pineapple Mini Pizzas

Take 2 purchased 30 cm round pizza bases (the thinner variety is best), and using a 6 cm biscuit cutter, cut rounds from each. Spread with $1/4$ cup pizza sauce, then top with 150 g sliced mozzarella, 100 g chopped sliced ham and $1/2$ cup drained crushed pineapple. Bake in preheated moderate 180°C oven for 15 minutes. Serve. Makes 30.

*Lower four clockwise from bottom left: Bacon Pizza Bites, Peperoni Rounds, Ham & Pineapple Mini Pizzas and Pissaladiere Squares*

3

# Pizza Basics

Ready-made pizza bases and sauces are available from many supermarkets. If you choose to make your own you can't go wrong with these simple recipes which are quick and easy to make.

## Pizza Base

*Preparation time:*
 20 minutes
*Total cooking time:*
 see individual recipes
*Makes one thick or two
 thin 30 cm pizza bases*

7 g sachet dry yeast
*1/2 teaspoon salt*
*1/2 teaspoon sugar*
*1 cup warm water*
*2 1/2 cups plain flour*
*2 tablespoons olive oil*
*2 teaspoons semolina
 or polenta*

1. Combine yeast, salt, sugar and water in a small bowl. Stand, covered with plastic wrap, in a warm place for 10 minutes or until mixture is foamy. Sift flour into a large bowl. Make a well in the centre, add the yeast mixture, mix to a dough.
2. Knead the dough on a lightly floured surface for 5 minutes or until smooth and elastic. For thick pizza, roll dough out to 35 cm round. For thin pizza, divide dough in half and roll out each portion to 35 cm round.
3. Brush a 30 cm pizza tray with oil, sprinkle with semolina or polenta. Place dough onto tray, tuck edges under to form a rim. Top and cook according to recipe.

*Stand the yeast mixture in a small bowl until foamy.*

*Tuck edges of dough under to form a rim.*

### Variations:
*For wholemeal pizza base*: Use 1 1/2 cups plain white flour and 1 cup plain wholemeal flour instead of plain flour.
*For cornmeal pizza base*: Use 2 cups of plain flour and 1/2 cup polenta (cornmeal) instead of plain flour.
**Note:** Dough may be made up to 1 day in advance. Place in an oiled bowl, cover with plastic wrap, and refrigerate until required. To use, allow dough to return to room temperature, knead gently for 2 minutes and shape as instructed. Dough may also be frozen if only one thin pizza is required. Place remaining dough in a freezer bag and seal tightly; freeze for up to 4 months. Thaw in the refrigerator overnight and allow to come to room temperature before shaping.

# Pizza Sauce

*Preparation time:*
  10 minutes
*Total cooking time:*
  15 minutes
*Makes 1½ cups sauce*

1 tablespoon olive oil
1 medium onion, finely
  chopped
2 cloves garlic, crushed
425 g can peeled
  tomatoes, crushed
1 teaspoon dried basil
1 teaspoon dried
  oregano
1 teaspoon sugar
salt and pepper to taste

**1.** Heat oil in medium
pan. Add onion and
stir-fry over low heat
for 5 minutes or until
very soft. Add crushed
garlic and cook for
1 minute.
**2.** Stir in tomato, herbs
and sugar and cook
over low heat for
10 minutes until
reduced and thickened.
Add salt and pepper, to
taste. Cool before use.

**Note:** Sauce may be
made up to 2 days in
advance. Place sauce in
an airtight container
and refrigerate until
required. The sauce
may also be frozen for
up to 2 months. You
may like to make a
double batch and freeze
the remaining sauce for
future use.

*Stir in tomato and herbs
to make thick sauce.*

---

*Even though you may buy bases and sauces it is fun and exciting to make your
own. That way you may use fresh ingredients like those shown above.*

# Pizzas

All your favourite pizzas are here, including Ham and Pineapple and Super Supreme. And you'll also find other wonderfully inventive toppings and pitta and focaccia bread used as bases.

## Super Supreme

*Preparation time:*
20 minutes
*Total cooking time:*
33 minutes
*Serves 4*

30 cm purchased pizza
  base
1 quantity purchased
  pizza sauce
1 tablespoon olive oil
1 medium green
  capsicum, chopped
100 g small button
  mushrooms, sliced
1 cup grated
  mozzarella cheese
45 g sliced ham
  cut into 1 cm strips
45 g cabanossi, thinly
  sliced
30 g sliced salami, cut
  into quarters
2 pineapple rings,
  drained and cut into
  chunks
2 tablespoons
  pitted black olives,
  sliced

**1.** Preheat oven to moderately hot 210°C (190°C Gas). Lightly oil 30 cm pizza tray. Place pizza base on prepared tray and spread evenly with sauce. Heat oil in frying pan, add capsicum and mushrooms, cook over medium heat for 2 minutes; set aside.
**2.** Sprinkle three-quarters of cheese over pizza base. Spoon the capsicum mixture over cheese. Arrange the ham, cabanossi, salami, pineapple and olives evenly over top. Sprinkle with the remaining cheese.
**3.** Bake for 30 minutes until base is crunchy and golden and cheese has melted. Cut into wedges and serve.

**Note:** Toppings can be adjusted to taste with additions such as chilli, anchovies, ground beef, or extra cheese.

*Super Supreme Pizza*

# Satay Chicken Pizzas

*Preparation time:*
20 minutes
*Total cooking time:*
25 minutes
*Serves 6*

2 chicken breast fillets
6 small oval pitta
  breads
1 medium red onion,
  finely sliced
400 g can baby corn,
  halved
¼ cup shredded fresh
  basil

**Satay Sauce**
2 teaspoons oil
1 small onion, finely
  chopped
¼ teaspoon turmeric
¼ teaspoon chilli
  powder
¼ teaspoon garlic
  powder
½ teaspoon soft brown
  sugar
2 teaspoons soy sauce
⅓ cup peanut butter
⅓ cup coconut milk

1. Preheat oven to moderately hot 210°C (190°C Gas). Trim the chicken of excess fat and sinew. Half fill a large frying pan with water and bring to boil. Add the chicken; reduce heat and simmer gently for 7 minutes, turning once during the cooking time. Remove the cooked chicken from pan and set aside to cool.
2. **To make satay sauce:** Heat oil in small pan, add onion and stir over low heat for 2 minutes. Add turmeric, chilli and garlic powders and cook, stirring, for 1 minute. Add sugar, soy sauce, peanut butter and coconut milk; stir over low heat for 1 minute until the ingredients are well combined. Transfer to bowl and set aside to cool.
3. Cut cooled chicken into thin slices. Reserve one-third of the satay sauce. Add chicken to remaining sauce and toss to coat lightly.
4. Spread pitta bread with reserved satay sauce. Arrange finely sliced red onion, baby corn spears and chicken mixture on pitta bases. Bake for 15 minutes or until bases are crisp. Sprinkle with fresh shredded basil. Serve.

**Note:** Pitta breads come in a variety of sizes and make excellent pizza bases.

*Seafood Pizza (top)
and Satay Chicken Pizzas*

# Seafood Pizza

*Preparation time:*
10 minutes
*Total cooking time:*
20 minutes
*Serves 4–6*

30 cm purchased pizza
  base
½ cup purchased pizza
  sauce
170 g can crabmeat,
  well drained
200 g peeled school
  prawns
105 g can oysters
¾ cup grated
  mozzarella cheese
freshly ground black
  pepper, to taste
1 tablespoon fresh
  oregano leaves

1. Preheat oven to moderately hot 210°C (190°C Gas). Place pizza base on oven tray, spread with sauce.
2. Spread drained crabmeat evenly over sauce. Scatter peeled prawns over crabmeat and arrange the oysters on top. Sprinkle with cheese.
3. Grind black pepper over the top of the prepared pizza. Bake for 20 minutes or until the cheese has melted and the pizza crust is crisp. Scatter with fresh oregano leaves, if desired. Serve immediately.

# Vegetarian Pizza

*Preparation time:*
20 minutes + base and
sauce
*Total cooking time:*
25 minutes
*Makes one 30 cm
pizza*

½ *quantity pizza sauce
(page 5)*
1 *thin cornmeal pizza
base (page 4)*
1 *small red capsicum,
finely chopped*
1 *small green capsicum,
finely chopped*
75 g *button
mushrooms, sliced*
1 *cup pineapple pieces,
well drained*
270 g *can corn kernels,
well drained*
1 *cup grated mozzarella
cheese*
1 *teaspoon dried mixed
Italian herbs*

1. Preheat oven to
moderately hot 210°C
(190°Gas). Spread
pizza sauce over base.
Sprinkle red and green
capsicum over the
sauce and arrange
mushrooms on top.
2. Spread pineapple
pieces and corn kernels
over mushrooms;
scatter cheese evenly
over pizza. Sprinkle
with herbs.
3. Bake for 25 minutes,
until crust is golden
brown. Allow to stand

for 5 minutes before
cutting into wedges to
serve.

# Super Meaty Pizza

*Preparation time:*
20 minutes + base and
sauce
*Total cooking time:*
35 minutes
*Serves 4–6*

4 *rashers bacon, cut
into 2 cm squares*
350 g *lean beef mince*
1 *quantity pizza sauce
(page 5)*
1 *thick pizza base
(page 4)*
100 g *sliced salami,
cut into wedges*
150 g *sliced ham, cut
into 2 cm squares*
1 *cup grated mozzarella
cheese*

1. Preheat oven to
moderately hot 210°C
(190°C Gas). Cook
bacon in a non-stick
frying pan over
medium heat for
4–5 minutes until just
browned. Remove from
pan; drain on paper
towel.
2. Add mince to pan.
Cook over medium
heat for 5 minutes until
meat is browned and
almost all liquid has
evaporated. Break up
any lumps with a fork
as it cooks. Add pizza
sauce to pan; combine

well. Transfer mixture
to a bowl to cool.
3. Spread cooled mince
mixture over pizza
base. Arrange bacon,
salami and ham over
mince; sprinkle with
cheese. Bake for
25 minutes, until crust
is golden brown. Allow
to stand for 5 minutes
before cutting into
wedges. Serve.

# Bacon & Egg
Pizza

*Preparation time:*
15 minutes
*Total cooking time:*
25 minutes
*Serves 4*

8 *rashers bacon*
1 *cup purchased pizza
sauce*
4 *purchased individual
pizza bases*
1 *cup grated cheddar
cheese*
4 *small eggs*
¼ *cup grated cheddar
cheese, extra*
*fresh oregano sprigs, to
garnish*

1. Preheat oven to
moderately hot 210°C
(190°C Gas). Remove
rind from bacon and
cut into 2 cm squares.
Heat a non-stick frying
pan and cook bacon
over medium heat for
5 minutes or until
lightly browned and

*Super Meaty Pizza (top), Bacon & Egg Pizza (centre) and Vegetarian Pizza*

crisp. Remove from pan and drain on paper towels.
2. Spread pizza sauce over bases; place on an oven tray. Divide bacon between bases and sprinkle with cheese. Make a small hollow in the cheese. Carefully break egg into the hollow, being careful to keep the yolk intact. Sprinkle each egg with extra grated cheese.
3. Bake for 20 minutes until egg is cooked, cheese has melted and crust is golden. Garnish with oregano, if desired, and serve.

# Deep Dish Pan Pizza

*Preparation time:*
15 minutes + base
and sauce
*Total cooking time:*
30 minutes
*Serves 4–6*

1 quantity pizza base
  dough, unrolled
  *(page 4)*
250 g pork and veal
  mince
½ quantity pizza sauce
  *(page 5)*
1 medium red capsicum,
  finely chopped
1 medium green
  capsicum, finely
  chopped
75 g button
  mushrooms, sliced
350 g plum (egg)
  tomatoes, sliced
⅓ cup stuffed green
  olives, sliced
1½ cups grated
  mozzarella cheese
½ cup shredded
  parmesan cheese
1 tablespoon olive oil

**1.** Preheat oven to
moderately hot 210°C
(190°C Gas). Brush a
26 cm springform tin
with oil. Coat base and
side with cornmeal,
shake out excess. Roll
out dough and line
base and about
three-quarters of the
way up the side of tin.
Fold edge over slightly
to form a rim.
**2.** Heat a non-stick
frying pan and add
mince. Cook over
medium heat for
3–5 minutes until
browned; use a fork to
break up any lumps as
it cooks. Drain off
excess liquid; cool.
**3.** Spread pizza sauce
onto the prepared base.
Top with mince and
scatter evenly with
finely chopped red and
green capsicum and
sliced button
mushrooms. Arrange
sliced plum tomato
attractively on top of
pizza. Sprinkle with
sliced green olives and
the mozzarella and
parmesan cheeses.
**4.** Brush rim of base
with olive oil. Bake for
25 minutes in a
moderately hot oven
until the cheese is
melted and pizza crust
is golden brown. Allow
pizza to stand 5 minutes
before cutting into
wedges. Serve
immediately.

**Note:** The crust for this
pizza is much thicker
than normal.

*Deep Dish Pan Pizza*

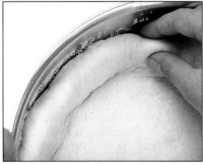

*Roll out dough and line base and side of
tin, folding edge of dough to form rim.*

*Use a fork to break up any lumps as the
meat is browning over medium heat.*

*Scatter chopped red and green capsicum and sliced mushrooms over mince.*

*After topping pizza with grated cheese, brush the rim of crust with oil.*

# Greek-Style Pizza

*Preparation time:*
20 minutes + sauce
*Total cooking time:*
20 minutes
*Serves 4*

1 bunch English
*spinach (500 g)*
50 g kalamata olives
*1/2 quantity pizza sauce*
*(page 5)*
4 x 17 cm pitta bread
*rounds*
*1/3 cup raisins*
*1/4 cup pine nuts*
200 g feta cheese

1. Preheat oven to
moderately hot 210°C
(190°C Gas). Remove
stalks from spinach and
discard; wash leaves
well in cold water.
Place in a large pan
with just the water
clinging to the leaves.
Cover and steam over
low heat, stirring
occasionally, until just
softened. Remove from
heat and cool.
2. Squeeze excess
moisture from spinach;
shred finely. Remove
stones from olives and
cut into quarters.
Spread pizza sauce onto
pitta breads; distribute
shredded spinach
evenly over sauce.
3. Sprinkle olives,
raisins and pine nuts
over spinach. Crumble
feta cheese over pizzas;
place onto oven trays.
Bake for 15 minutes, or
until the cheese is
golden and the bases
are crisp. Serve
immediately.

# Goats Cheese &
Vegetable Pizza

*Preparation time:*
30 minutes + base
*Total cooking time:*
35 minutes
*Serves 4–6*

1 medium red caspicum
*2 teaspoons oil*
1 small onion, finely
*chopped*
2 cloves garlic, crushed
*2 medium zucchini*
2 medium slender
*eggplant*
2 medium tomatoes,
*sliced*
1 thin pizza base
*(page 4)*
*1/4 cup finely shredded*
*fresh basil*
salt and pepper
100 g sweet potato,
*finely sliced*
olive oil, extra
100 g goats cheese
*(chevre), sliced*

1. Preheat oven to
moderately hot 210°C
(190°C Gas). Cut
capsicum in quarters
lengthways. Remove
seeds and membrane,
place skin side up on a
flat tray and cook
under a hot grill for
5 minutes, until skin
turns black. Remove
from heat, cover with a
clean tea towel, and
allow to cool. When
cold, peel off skins and
cut flesh in 1 cm strips.
2. Heat oil in a small
pan. Cook onion over
low heat for 4 minutes,
until soft. Add garlic
and cook 1 minute
further. Cool.
3. Using a vegetable
peeler, peel zucchini
and eggplant into long
thin strips, then cut
strips in half crossways.
Arrange tomato on
pizza base; spread
onion mixture over
tomato. Sprinkle with
shredded basil, salt and
pepper.
4. Arrange sweet
potato, zucchini and
eggplant on pizza;
brush lightly with olive
oil. Add the capsicum
and goats cheese over
top. Brush crust rim
lightly with olive oil.
Bake for 25 minutes,
until crust is golden.
Cut into wedges and
serve immediately.

**Note:** Goats cheese has
quite a pungent flavour
that does not appeal to
all. Substitute feta
cheese, if desired.

---

*Greek-Style Pizza (top) and Goats Cheese &*
*Vegetable Pizza*

# Santa Fe Spicy Pizza

*Preparation time:*
15 minutes + base
*Total cooking time:*
25 minutes
*Serves 4*

350 g plum tomatoes,
  finely chopped
3 spring onions, finely
  sliced
2 tablespoons finely
  chopped fresh
  coriander
1 tablespoon olive oil
1 teaspoon red wine
  vinegar
1 clove crushed garlic
1 thin cornmeal pizza
  base (page 4)
60 g hot Spanish
  salami, cut into short
  thin strips
1/4 cup sliced bottled
  jalapeno peppers,
  drained
3/4 cup grated cheddar
  cheese
oregano leaves, to
  garnish

1. Preheat oven to
moderately hot 210°C
(190°C Gas). Combine
the tomato, spring
onion, coriander, oil,
vinegar and crushed
garlic in a small bowl;
leave to stand for
10 minutes.
2. Drain tomato
mixture and spread
over pizza base. Scatter
salami and peppers
evenly over top, and
sprinkle with cheddar
cheese. Bake pizza for
25 minutes, until the
crust is golden and
crisp. Garnish with
oregano, if desired. Cut
into wedges, and serve
immediately.

# BBQ Chicken Pizza

*Preparation time:*
20 minutes + base and
sauce
*Total cooking time:*
25 minutes
*Serves 4*

1/2 quantity cornmeal
  pizza base dough,
  unrolled (page 4)
1/2 quantity pizza sauce
  (page 5)
1/4 cup barbecue sauce
1/2 purchased barbecued
  chicken
1 medium red onion,
  sliced
1 cup grated gruyère
  cheese
80 g cherry tomatoes,
  quartered
1 tablespoon olive oil
1 tablespoon chopped
  fresh parsley

1. Preheat oven to
moderately hot 210°C
(190°C Gas). Brush
2 oven trays with oil,
sprinkle with cornmeal.
Divide the dough in
half and roll out to
2 x 17 cm rounds;
place onto prepared
trays. Combine pizza
sauce with barbecue
sauce and mix well.
Spread onto bases.
2. Remove all meat
from chicken. Discard
bones, shred meat into
pieces. Scatter onion
onto pizza bases, top
with half the cheese.
Spread chicken evenly
over cheese, and
arrange tomato on top.
3. Spread the remaining
cheese over pizzas.
Brush crust rim with
olive oil; bake for
25 minutes until
golden. Sprinkle with
chopped parsley and
serve.

# Four Cheese Pizza

*Preparation time:*
15 minutes + base and
sauce
*Total cooking time:*
10 minutes
*Serves 4–6*

125 g camembert
  cheese
150 g blue vein
  cheese
100 g bocconcini
  cheese
1/2 quantity pizza sauce
  (page 5)
26 cm round purchased
  pizza base
1/3 cup shredded
  parmesan cheese
1 teaspoon olive oil

*From top: Santa Fe Spicy Pizza, Four Cheese Pizza, BBQ Chicken Pizza*

**1.** Preheat oven to moderately hot 210°C (190°C Gas). Chop camembert cheese into 1 cm cubes; crumble the blue vein cheese and thinly slice the bocconcini.

**2.** Spread pizza sauce over base; scatter camembert and blue vein over sauce. Arrange the slices of bocconcini on top of the pizza and sprinkle with parmesan. Brush dough rim with oil.

**3.** Bake for 10 minutes, until cheeses have melted. Allow to stand for 5 minutes. Serve.

17

*Bigger Than Texas*

*Prepare a non-stick tray. Brush with oil and sprinkle with polenta or semolina.*

*Add sauce and kidney beans to pan with softened onion and browned mince.*

18

# Bigger than Texas

*Preparation time:*
  *20 minutes + base*
*Total cooking time:*
  *30 minutes*
*Serves 6–8*

2 teaspoons oil
1 medium onion, finely
  chopped
500 g lean beef mince
1½ cups chunky taco
  sauce
425 g can kidney
  beans, rinsed and
  drained
1 quantity pizza base
  dough, unrolled
  (page 4)
1 cup grated mozzarella
  cheese
2 medium avocados,
  sliced
½ cup sour cream

**1.** Preheat oven to moderately hot 210°C (190°C Gas). Brush a (25 cm x 38 cm) non-stick tray with oil; sprinkle with polenta or semolina.
**2.** Heat oil in frying pan, add onion and cook over moderate heat for 2 minutes until soft. Add mince, cook for 5 minutes until the mince is browned and almost all the liquid has evaporated. Add taco sauce and kidney beans to pan; stir to combine. Transfer mixture to a bowl to cool.
**3.** Roll out dough to a 25 cm x 38 cm rectangle. Place on prepared tray; tuck edges under to form a rim. Spread cooled mince mixture onto base; sprinkle with cheese. Bake for 25 minutes until the crust is golden brown.
**4.** Arrange the avocado slices in two rows along the length of pizza. Cut the pizza into squares and serve immediately with a dollop of sour cream.

*Place dough on tray, tucking under edge, and spread with cooled mince mixture.*

*When the pizza is cooked place two rows of sliced avocado evenly on top.*

# Individual Pesto Pizzas

*Preparation time:*
20 minutes + base
*Total cooking time:*
20 minutes
*Serves 6*

½ *quantity pizza base
dough, unrolled
(page 4)*
6 *slices prosciutto,
cut crossways into
2 cm strips*
6 *artichoke hearts,
quartered*
100 g *bocconcini,
sliced*

**Pesto**
1 *cup firmly packed
fresh basil leaves*
¼ *cup pine nuts*
2 *cloves garlic*
¼ *cup shredded
parmesan cheese*
⅓ *cup olive oil*

1. Preheat oven to
moderately hot 210°C
(190°C Gas). Brush
2 oven trays with oil,
sprinkle with polenta
or semolina. Divide
dough into 6 portions;
roll out each one to a
13 cm round.
2. **To make pesto:** Place
basil, pine nuts, garlic
and cheese into food
processor. Process
1 minute, until well
chopped. With motor
running, add oil in a
thin stream; process
until mixture is
smooth.
3. Spread each round
with pesto. Arrange
prosciutto, artichokes
and bocconcini onto
the bases. Bake for
20 minutes, until cheese
has melted and bases
are golden and crisp.
Serve immediately.

# Onion-olive Pizza

*Preparation time:*
25 minutes + base
*Total cooking time:*
55 minutes
*Serves 4*

2 *tablespoons olive oil*
3 *large onions, sliced*
2 *large red capsicums*
¾ *cup pitted kalamata
olives*
2 *cloves garlic, crushed*
1 *tablespoon capers*
¼ *cup olive oil, extra*
½ *quantity pizza base
dough, unrolled
(page 4)*
½ *cup grated parmesan
cheese*

1. Preheat oven to
moderately hot 210°C
(190°C Gas). Brush
2 oven trays with oil;
sprinkle with semolina
or polenta. Heat oil in
large pan. Add onion;
cook over low heat for
15 minutes until very
soft, stirring
occasionally. Increase
heat to medium, cook
further 15 minutes until
golden. Set aside to
cool.
2. Cut capsicum in
quarters lengthways.
Remove seeds and
membrane; place skin
side up on a flat tray
and cook under a hot
grill for 5 minutes until
skin turns black.
Remove from heat,
cover with a clean tea
towel and allow to
cool. When cold peel
off skins and cut into
1 cm strips.
3. Place olives, garlic
and capers in food
processor. Process for
30 seconds. With motor
running, add oil in a
thin stream until
mixture is smooth.
Divide dough into
quarters; roll out each
portion to a 15 cm
square. Spread olive
mixture onto bases,
leaving a 2 cm border;
place onto prepared
trays.
4. Spread onions over
olive paste, sprinkle
with cheese. Arrange
capsicum strips
diagonally over onion.
Bake for 20 minutes
until crust is golden.
Cut into wedges and
serve immediately.

*Onion-olive Pizza (top) and Individual
Pesto Pizzas*

# Tomato & Mozzarella Pizza

*Preparation time:*
15 minutes
*Total cooking time:*
25 minutes
*Serves 2*

250 g cherry tomatoes,
   halved
4 bocconcini cheeses,
   cut into quarters
1 clove garlic, crushed
1 tablespoon olive oil
24 cm oval focaccia
   bread
½ quantity pizza sauce
   (page 5)
salt and ground black
   pepper
2 teaspoons fresh
   oregano leaves
1 teaspoon fresh
   rosemary sprigs

**1.** Preheat oven to moderately hot 210°C (190°C Gas). Combine tomato, bocconcini, garlic and oil in a medium bowl and mix well.
**2.** Place focaccia bread on a baking tray, spread with sauce and bake for 5 minutes. Remove from oven; top with tomato and bocconcini mixture and sprinkle with salt and pepper, to taste. Bake for 20 minutes or until focaccia is crunchy and cheese has melted. Sprinkle with oregano and rosemary. Cut into wedges and serve immediately.

# Marinated Feta Pizza

*Preparation time:*
20 minutes + base
*Total cooking time:*
25 minutes
*Serves 4–6*

¾ cup sundried
   tomatoes
1 clove garlic, crushed
1 tablespoon pine nuts
¼ cup olive oil
200 g English spinach
1 thin wholemeal pizza
   base (page 4)
1 medium red onion,
   finely sliced
2 medium tomatoes,
   cut into wedges
8 anchovy fillets, finely
   sliced
150 g marinated feta
   cheese, drained and
   crumbled

**1.** Preheat oven to moderately hot 210°C (190°C Gas). Place sundried tomato in a small bowl and cover with boiling water. Stand for 5 minutes; drain well. Combine the sundried tomato, garlic and pine nuts in food processor. Process for 20 seconds or until well chopped. With motor running add oil in a thin stream and process until mixture is smooth.
**2.** Remove stalks from spinach and discard, wash leaves well in cold water. Place in a large pan with just the water clinging to the leaves. Cover and steam over low heat, stirring occasionally, until just softened. Remove from heat; cool and dry on paper towels.
**3.** Spread sundried tomato mixture onto pizza base. Arrange a layer of whole spinach leaves on top. Sprinkle with finely sliced red onion; cut tomato wedges into quarters and arrange on top.
**4.** Place anchovies evenly over topping; add crumbled feta. Bake for 25 minutes until crust is golden brown. Cut pizza into wedges and serve immediately.

*Marinated Feta Pizza (top) and Tomato &*
*Mozzarella Pizza*

## Peperoni Pizza

*Preparation time:*
15 minutes
*Total cooking time:*
20 minutes
*Serves 4*

30 cm purchased pizza
   base
1 quantity purchased
   pizza sauce
1 cup grated mozzarella
   or cheddar cheese
80 g peperoni, thinly
   sliced
50 g salami, thinly
   sliced
40 g mortadella, cut
   into quarters

1. Preheat oven to
moderately hot 210°C
(190°C Gas). Place
pizza base on a lightly
oiled pizza tray.
2. Spread pizza evenly
with sauce. Sprinkle
with 3/4 cup mozzarella
or cheddar cheese.
Arrange the peperoni,
salami and mortadella
on top and sprinkle
remaining cheese over
pizza.
3. Bake in oven for
20 minutes or until
cheese has melted and
base is crunchy and
golden. Cut into
wedges and serve.

**Note:** Other meats may
be used: try pancetta,
prosciutto and assorted
hot or spicy salamis.

## Lemon Scallop Pizza

*Preparation time:*
25 minutes + base
*Total cooking time:*
35 minutes
*Serves 4*

150 g scallops
1 1/2 cups water
1 tablespoon lemon
   juice
1 tablespoon butter
2 sprigs lemon thyme
1 tablespoon olive oil
25 g prosciutto, cut
   into 1 cm strips
1 thin pizza base
   (page 4)
100 g mozzarella cheese
   cut into 5 mm slices
2 teaspoons finely
   chopped fresh lemon
   thyme
2 teaspoons finely
   chopped fresh chives

**Sauce:**
1 tablespoon olive oil
1 clove garlic, crushed
2 spring onions, chopped
3 large ripe tomatoes,
   peeled, seeded and
   chopped
1 teaspoon grated
   lemon rind
salt and pepper, to taste

1. Preheat oven to
moderately hot 210°C
(190°C Gas). Clean and
remove vein from
scallops. Heat water in
a medium pan; add
lemon juice, butter
and sprigs of lemon
thyme. Bring to boil,
reduce heat, add
scallops and simmer
gently for 2 minutes.
Remove with slotted
spoon, drain on paper
towels and set aside.
Heat oil in a frying pan
and cook prosciutto
over moderate heat for
2 minutes. Remove
from pan and drain on
paper towels.
2. **To make sauce**: Heat
1 tablespoon olive oil
in medium pan. Add
garlic and onion; cook
over low heat for
2 minutes. Add tomato
and rind; cook for
further 6 minutes until
sauce is reduced. Add
pepper and salt. Remove
from heat and cool.
3. Spread the sauce
evenly over the pizza
base. Arrange
mozzarella slices on top
with the scallops and
prosciutto; sprinkle
with chopped lemon
thyme and chives. Bake
for 25 minutes until
crust is golden brown.
Cut into wedges. Serve.

**Note:** Poaching the
scallops prevents them
becoming too dry
during later cooking.

*Peperoni Pizza (top)
and Lemon Scallop Pizza*

# Smoked Salmon Pizza

*Preparation time:*
25 minutes + base
*Total cooking time:*
35 minutes
*Serves 4*

*½ quantity pizza base
dough (page 4)*
*¼ cup olive oil*
*2 large ripe tomatoes,
thinly sliced*
*180 g cream cheese,
sliced*
*1 medium red onion,
cut into thin wedges*
*100 g smoked salmon*
*1 tablespoon lemon
juice*
*1 tablespoon capers*
*2 teaspoons finely
chopped fresh dill*
*pepper, to taste*

1. Preheat oven to
moderately hot 210°C
(190°C Gas). Brush a
30 cm pizza tray with
oil and sprinkle with
polenta. Roll out pizza
dough to 30 cm circle
and place on prepared
tray. Brush with a little
olive oil and sprinkle
with salt. Prick dough
with a fork. Bake for
20 minutes.
2. Arrange tomato
slices, cream cheese and
onion wedges on pizza
base. Bake in oven for
15 minutes until crust
is golden brown.

3. Sprinkle smoked
salmon with lemon
juice. Stand for
5 minutes, then arrange
on pizza base. Sprinkle
with capers and finely
chopped dill, if desired.
Add pepper, to taste.
Cut into wedges and
serve at once.

# Mushroom Pizza

*Preparation time:*
25 minutes + base
*Total cooking time:*
45–50 minutes
*Serves 4*

*2 tablespoons olive oil*
*2 tablespoons finely
chopped spring onions*
*275 g button
mushrooms, wiped
and sliced*
*150 g oyster
mushrooms, sliced*
*1 thin pizza base
(page 4)*
*125 g mozzarella
cheese, cut into thin
slices*
*1 tablespoon chopped
fresh coriander*

*Sauce*
*1 tablespoon olive oil*
*2 cloves garlic, crushed*
*1 tablespoon tomato
paste*
*475 g can tomatoes,
crushed*
*1 teaspoon sugar*

*1 teaspoon ground
coriander*
*½ teaspoon ground
cumin*
*¼ teaspoon sweet
paprika*
*salt and pepper*

1. Preheat oven to
moderate 210°C
(190°C Gas). Heat
2 tablespoons oil in
frying pan, add spring
onion and mushrooms;
cook over low heat for
4 minutes. Remove
from heat; drain on
paper towels.
2. **To make sauce:** Heat
oil in medium pan, add
garlic, cook for
2 minutes. Stir in
tomato paste, cook for
1 minute. Add tomato,
sugar, coriander, cumin,
paprika, and salt and
pepper to taste. Bring to
boil, reduce heat and
simmer 20 minutes or
until sauce is reduced.
Remove from heat and
set aside.
3. Spread base with
prepared sauce.
Arrange the sliced
mozzarella cheese
evenly over sauce and
top with mushroom
mixture; sprinkle with
the finely chopped
coriander. Bake pizza in
oven for 25 minutes
until crust is golden
brown. Cut pizza into
wedges and serve.

*Smoked Salmon Pizza (top)
and Mushroom Pizza*

## Garlic Prawn & Potato Pizza

*Preparation time:*
40 minutes + base
*Total cooking time:*
1 1/2 hours
*Serves 4*

2 medium potatoes,
    unpeeled and cut into
    eight wedges
oil for brushing
salt
1 large red capsicum
375 g (12) medium
    green prawns
2 tablespoons olive oil,
    extra
3 cloves garlic, crushed
1 small red chilli, finely
    chopped
1 thin pizza base
    (page 4)
125g mozzarella
    cheese, cut into thin
    rounds
1/4 cup fresh basil,
    shredded

**Sauce**
50 g sundried tomatoes
1 cup boiling water
1 medium ripe tomato,
    peeled, seeded and
    chopped
2 tablespoons olive oil

**1.** Preheat oven to
moderately hot, 210°C
(190°C Gas). Brush
potato wedges with oil;
place on a baking tray
and sprinkle with salt.
Bake for 30 minutes

until cooked through.
Cool slightly, scoop out
flesh and set skins
aside.
**2.** Cut capsicum in half,
remove seeds and
membrane; place skin
side up on grill tray and
cook under preheated
grill for 5–7 minutes, or
until the skin blisters
and turns black.
Remove from heat,
cover with a clean tea
towel and allow to
cool. When cool peel
off skins and cut flesh
into 1 cm strips. Set
aside.
**3.** Peel and devein the
prawns, leaving tails
intact. Heat oil in a
non-stick frying pan.
Add garlic and
1/2 teaspoon chilli and
cook for 1–2 minutes;
add prawns and cook
over medium heat for
1 minute on each side.
Remove and set aside.
**4. To make sauce:** Place
sundried tomatoes and
boiling water in a small
bowl. Stand for
8 minutes and allow
tomatoes to become
soft; drain. Place
drained tomato,
chopped tomato and
olive oil in a food
processor. Process to a
smooth paste.
**5.** Spread sauce evenly
over pizza base;
arrange rounds of
mozzarella cheese over
the sauce. Top with
prepared prawns,

capsicum strips and
potato skins. Sprinkle
generously with
shredded basil and
remaining chilli. Bake
for 35 minutes until
crust is golden. Cut
into wedges and serve
immediately.

## Pizza Pockets

*Preparation time:*
20 minutes
*Total cooking time:*
20 minutes
*Makes 2*

1/2 quantity pizza base
    dough (page 4)
1 cup grated mozzarella
    cheese
2 medium ripe
    tomatoes, thinly sliced
1 medium red onion,
    thinly sliced
100 g ham off the
    bone, cut into cubes
2 teaspoons dried
    oregano
salt and pepper
1 cup grated cheddar
    cheese
oil for brushing

**1.** Preheat oven to
moderately hot, 210°C
(190°C Gas). Brush a
30 cm pizza tray with
oil and sprinkle with
polenta. Divide pizza
dough into two
portions. Roll pizza
dough into two 24 cm
circles. On one half of
each of the circles

*Pizza Pockets (top) and Garlic Prawn & Potato Pizza*

sprinkle 1/2 cup of mozzarella cheese, half the tomato, half of the onion, and half the cubed ham. Sprinkle with oregano, salt and pepper. Top with cheddar cheese.

**2.** Brush the edge of each pizza base with oil and fold the plain half over to form a semi-circle. Pinch the edges firmly together. Place both pizza pockets on the prepared tray and

brush with olive oil. Sprinkle lightly with salt. Bake the pizzas for 20 minutes or until golden and crisp. Cut the pizza pockets in half and serve immediately.

29

# Ham & Pineapple Pizza

*Preparation time:*
  *25 minutes + sauce*
*Total cooking time:*
  *25 minutes*
*Serves 4*

*1 ½ cups self raising*
  *flour*
*30 g butter*
*½ cup milk*
*½ quantity pizza sauce*
  *(page 5)*
*1 ½ cups grated*
  *mozzarella cheese*
*150 g ham off the*
  *bone, chopped in*
  *cubes*
*225 g can pineapple*
  *rings, well drained*

**1.** Preheat oven to moderately hot 210°C (190°C Gas). Brush a 30 cm pizza tray with oil. Place flour and butter in a food processor; process 20 seconds or until mixture resembles fine breadcrumbs. Add milk, process a further 30 seconds or until mixture just comes together. Turn onto a lightly floured surface, knead gently for 1 minute or until smooth. Roll out to 30 cm circle. Place on prepared tray and fold edges inwards to form a rim.

**2.** Spread pizza sauce over the base and sprinkle with 1 cup of the grated mozzarella cheese. Top with ham cubes. Cut pineapple rings into pieces and scatter over top of pizza. Sprinkle with remaining cheese.

**3.** Bake for 25 minutes or until pastry crust is golden brown. Cut into wedges and serve immediately.

# Super Seafood Pizza

*Preparation time:*
  *35 minutes + base*
*Total cooking time:*
  *40 minutes*
*Serves 4*

*250 g green prawns*
*80 g scallops*
*150 g baby octopus*
*200 g mussels in shell*
*1 ½ cups water*
*½ cup white wine*
*½ teaspoon chopped*
  *fresh chilli*
*1 thin pizza base*
  *( page 4)*
*1 cup grated mozzarella*
  *cheese*
*1 tablespoon capers*
*1 tablespoon finely*
  *chopped fresh parsley*

***Sauce***
*1 tablespoon olive oil*
*1 clove garlic, crushed*
*2 tablespoons spring*
  *onions, finely chopped*

*1 tablespoon tomato*
  *paste*
*3 large ripe tomatoes,*
  *peeled, seeded and*
  *chopped*
*1 tablespoon sweet*
  *sherry*
*1 tablespoon finely*
  *chopped fresh parsley*

**1.** Preheat oven to moderately hot 210°C (190°C Gas). Peel and devein prawns. Clean and remove vein from scallops. Clean octopus; remove beak and insides and cut flesh into halves. Scrub mussels and remove beards. Heat water, wine and chilli in a medium pan. Bring to boil, reduce heat to simmer. Add prawns and cook gently for 2 minutes; remove with a slotted spoon; drain. Add scallops and cook gently for 1 ½ minutes, remove with slotted spoon; drain. Add octopus and cook gently for 2 minutes, remove with a slotted spoon; drain. Add mussels, cover pan with lid and steam for 3 minutes until shells are open, discarding any mussels that do not open. Remove mussel from shell, if desired, or leave in shell. Set seafood aside.

**2. *To make sauce:*** Heat oil in medium pan, add garlic and spring onion

*Ham & Pineapple Pizza (top) and Super Seafood Pizza*

and cook over low heat for 2 minutes. Add tomato paste, and cook stirring constantly 1 minute; add tomato, sherry and chopped parsley. Simmer for 6 minutes or until the sauce has thickened and reduced a little. Remove from heat and allow to cool.
**3.** Spread sauce evenly over the pizza base. Sprinkle with cheese. Arrange seafood over cheese. Sprinkle with capers and parsley. Bake for 30 minutes until crust is golden brown. Serve.

31

## Vegetable Pizza

*Preparation time:*
20 minutes + base and
sauce
*Total cooking time:*
25 minutes
*Serves 4–6*

100 g broccoli, cut into
   small florets
1 bunch asparagus
   spears, cut into 3 cm
   lengths
1 medium carrot, cut
   into matchsticks
½ quantity pizza sauce
   (page 5)
1 thin wholemeal pizza
   base (page 4)
2 medium zucchini, cut
   into matchsticks
130 g can corn kernels,
   well drained
½ cup beansprouts
2 medium tomatoes,
   chopped
¾ cup grated low fat
   cheddar cheese

1. Preheat oven to
moderately hot 210°C
(190°C Gas). Place
broccoli, asparagus and
carrot in a large
heatproof bowl. Cover
with boiling water,
stand 2 minutes. Drain,
plunge into iced water
and drain again. Pat
dry with paper towels.
2. Spread pizza sauce
onto base. Arrange
broccoli, asparagus,
carrot and zucchini
over sauce. Sprinkle

corn kernels over, then
beansprouts and top
with tomato.
3. Sprinkle pizza with
cheese. Bake pizza for
25 minutes until cheese
has melted and the
crust is golden. Serve.

## Italian Salami Pizza

*Preparation time:*
20 minutes + base
*Total cooking time:*
40 minutes
*Serves 4*

**Sauce**
1 tablespoon olive oil
2 cloves garlic, crushed
1 red chilli, finely
   chopped
1 tablespoon tomato
   paste
400 g can tomatoes,
   crushed
¼ teaspoon sweet
   paprika
1 tablespoon dried
   oregano
2 large fresh basil
   leaves, shredded
1 teaspoon coarse black
   pepper
salt, to taste
1 thin pizza base
   (page 4)
150 g mozzarella
   cheese, cut into
   5 mm slices
12–14 thin slices Italian
   salami

45 g can anchovy
   fillets, drained and
   thinly sliced
1 cup pitted black
   olives
fresh oregano leaves, to
   garnish

1. Preheat oven to
moderately hot 210°C
(190°C Gas).
*To make sauce:* Heat
oil in medium pan, add
crushed garlic and chilli
and cook over medium
heat for 1 minute.
Add tomato paste and
cook 1 minute further.
Stir in tomato, paprika,
oregano, basil, pepper
and salt. Bring to the
boil and simmer gently
over low heat for
12 minutes. Remove
from heat and cool.
2. Spread the cooled
sauce over the pizza
base and arrange the
cheese, salami, thinly
sliced anchovies and
olives on top of the
sauce. Bake for
25 minutes, until crust
is golden brown.
Garnish with oregano
leaves, if desired. Cut
into wedges and serve
immediately.

**Note:** Italian salami
comes in many
different flavours. Use
your favourite salami
or try new tastes for
variety.

*Italian Salami Pizza (top)
and Vegetable Pizza*

# Apple & Ginger Dessert Pizza

*Preparation time:*
35 minutes
*Total cooking time:*
30 minutes
*Serves 6*

**Base**
2 teaspoons dried yeast
2 teaspoons sugar
1/3 cup warm water
1 1/2 cups plain flour
25 g soft butter
1 egg, lightly beaten

**Topping**
1/2 cup sultanas
2 tablespoons brandy
30 g butter
1 1/2 teaspoons ground
ginger
2 tablespoons water
2 tablespoons maple
syrup
1 medium red apple,
cored and cut into
wedges
1 medium green apple,
cored and cut into
wedges
2 teaspoons melted
butter
thick cream, to serve

**1. To make base:**
Combine yeast, sugar
and water in a small
bowl. Stand bowl,
covered with plastic
wrap, in a warm place
for 10 minutes until
mixture is foamy.
**2.** Sift flour into large
bowl and make a well
in centre. Add yeast
mixture, butter and
egg; mix with knife to a
soft dough. Turn out
onto a lightly floured
surface; knead for
5 minutes until smooth
and elastic. Place in an
oiled bowl, cover with
plastic wrap; stand in
warm place for 1 hour
or until dough is
doubled in size.
**3. To make topping:**
Combine sultanas and
brandy in small bowl;
set aside. Melt butter in
pan, add ginger; stir to
combine. Add water
and maple syrup; cook
over low heat for
4 minutes until
thickened slightly. Cool.
**4.** Preheat oven to
moderately hot 210°C
(190°C Gas). Brush a
30 cm round pizza tray
with melted butter.
Knead dough again for
1 minute, roll out to a
26 cm round. Place
onto prepared tray,
tuck edges under to
form a rim. Drain
sultanas, sprinkle over
base. Arrange apple
slices on top, drizzle
with syrup. Brush rim
of pastry with a little
melted butter. Bake for
25 minutes until crust
is golden brown. Serve
warm with thick cream.

# Blueberry-banana Dessert Pizza

*Preparation time:*
30 minutes
*Total cooking time:*
25 minutes
*Serves 6*

**Base**
1 1/2 cups plain flour
30 g butter
1/2 cup milk

**Topping**
1/2 cup mascarpone
cheese
2 teaspoons demerara
sugar
2 small bananas, sliced
200 g punnet
blueberries
1/2 cup chopped pecans
2 teaspoons demerara
sugar, extra
2 teaspoons melted
butter

**1. To make base:**
Preheat oven to
moderately hot 210°C
(190°C Gas). Brush a
30 cm pizza tray with
melted butter. Place
flour and butter in a
food processor bowl;
process 20 seconds or
until mixture resembles
fine breadcrumbs. Add
milk, process further
30 seconds until
mixture comes together.
Turn out onto a lightly
floured surface, knead
gently for 1 minute

*Apple & Ginger Dessert Pizza (top) and Blueberry-banana Dessert Pizza*

until smooth. Roll out to 28 cm; place onto prepared tray and fold edges inward to form a rim.

**2. *To make topping:*** Spread mascarpone over base, sprinkle with sugar. Arrange sliced banana in ring along the edge of the pizza and in smaller ring towards the centre. Fill the inside of rings with blueberries.

**3.** Sprinkle with pecans and extra sugar. Brush pastry rim with a little melted butter. Bake for 25 minutes until pastry crust is golden. Serve warm with cream or ice-cream, if desired.

35

# Melts

Delicious breads and cheeses are readily available from supermarkets and delicatessens today, and these two ingredients are an essential part of the melts in this book. The following recipes will show you how to combine them with a variety of foods, resulting in tasty meals that are easy to prepare and suitable for many different occasions.

## B.L.T. with Cheese

*Preparation time:*
15 minutes
*Total cooking time:*
10 minutes
*Serves 2*

4 *thin rashers of bacon*
8 *thick slices white bread*
50 *g butter*
4 *slices cheddar cheese*
4 *cos lettuce leaves, shredded*
1 *large ripe tomato, thinly sliced*
2 *tablespoons tomato sauce*
*pepper*
*potato crisps, to garnish*

**1.** Cook bacon under a preheated grill for 2–3 minutes each side, according to taste. Toast the bread on both sides until lightly browned. Spread with butter, if desired.
**2.** Place cheese on 4 slices of toast. Cook under grill until cheese melts. Top remaining toast slices with lettuce, tomato and grilled bacon. Drizzle with tomato sauce and sprinkle with pepper. Place one slice on each of 4 serving plates and top with remaining toast slices with the cheese side down. Garnish with potato crisps and serve.

**Note:** This bacon, lettuce and tomato sandwich, invented in the United States, is known as a B.L.T. throughout the world.

*From top: Chicken & Asparagus Melt (see recipe next page) and B.L.T. with Cheese*

# Chicken & Asparagus Melt

*Preparation time:*
15 minutes
*Total cooking time:*
7 minutes
*Serves 4*

4 slices thick
  wholegrain bread
50 g butter
½ purchased barbecued
  chicken
340 g can asparagus
  spears, drained
125 g camembert
  cheese, sliced

**1.** Preheat grill to moderately hot. Toast bread lightly on both sides until golden. Spread one side of toast with butter, if desired.
**2.** Remove meat from chicken and shred coarsely. Divide shredded chicken equally on toast slices. Arrange asparagus spears over chicken, trimming the asparagus if necessary.
**3.** Lay camembert slices on top of chicken and asparagus. Place under the grill and cook for 5 minutes until cheese has melted and chicken is heated through. Serve immediately.

# Eggplant 'Sandwiches'

*Preparation time:*
20 minutes + standing
*Total cooking time:*
20 minutes
*Serves 4*

1 large eggplant
salt
2 tablespoons olive oil
⅓ cup ricotta cheese
1 medium tomato,
  thickly sliced
¼ cup shredded fresh
  basil leaves
¼ cup grated parmesan
  cheese
¼ cup fresh
  breadcrumbs

**1.** Cut eggplant into 8 slices, about 1 cm thick. Arrange in a single layer on a tray or board and sprinkle generously with salt. Stand for 20 minutes; rinse under cold water and pat dry with paper towels.
**2.** Preheat oven to moderately hot 210°C (190°C Gas). Brush an oven tray with oil. Lay 4 slices of eggplant on prepared tray; brush with oil. Spread ricotta onto each slice; top with slice of tomato and basil.

**3.** Place another eggplant slice on each stack. Brush lightly with olive oil; sprinkle with combined parmesan cheese and breadcrumbs. Bake for 20 minutes until eggplant is tender and golden. Serve immediately.

# Ploughman's Corned Beef

*Preparation time:*
15 minutes
*Total cooking time:*
5 minutes
*Serves 2*

2 wholegrain rolls
2 teaspoons wholegrain
  mustard
¼ cup bread and butter
  cucumber pickles
1 large ripe tomato,
  thinly sliced
125 g sliced corned
  beef
2 cups grated edam
  cheese

**1.** Split rolls in half horizontally and toast each side lightly until golden.
**2.** Spread bottom half of each roll with mustard and pickles. Top with tomato, corned beef and cheese. Place under preheated grill for 2 minutes or until cheese has melted. Cover with remaining tops. Serve.

*Eggplant Sandwich (top)*
*and Ploughman's Corned Beef*

# Panfried Ham & Cheese Sandwich

*Preparation time:*
  10 minutes
*Total cooking time:*
  5 minutes
*Serves 2*

4 thick slices white high
  top loaf
60 g soft butter
2 teaspoons wholegrain
  mustard
4 slices leg ham
60 g gruyère cheese,
  sliced

**1.** Spread one side of each bread slice completely with butter, making sure to include the crust. Place the buttered side of two slices lightly together. Spread mustard onto unbuttered side of top slice. Lay a slice of ham over the mustard; add a layer of cheese slices.

**2.** Preheat large frying pan. When hot gently lift top slice of bread with filling and place butter side down into pan. Top with other slice, with the butter side up.

**3.** Cook over medium heat for 2 minutes until underside is golden and cheese is beginning to melt. Using a spatula, carefully turn sandwich over to cook on other side. Lift onto a plate and carefully cut in half diagonally. Repeat the same process with the remaining sandwich. Serve sandwiches immediately.

**Note:** It is important to have the heat just at medium level. If it is too hot, the bread will burn before the cheese melts.

*Panfried Ham & Cheese Sandwich*

*Thoroughly butter one side of each bread slice right out to the crust edge.*

*Place slice of ham and layer of cheese slices on bread spread with mustard.*

*Lay bread with topping in pan and cover with other slice buttered side up.*

*When first side is cooked gently turn sandwich and cook on other side.*

# Mushroom & Bacon Croissant

*Preparation time:*
10 minutes
*Total cooking time:*
20 minutes
*Serves 4*

4 rashers bacon
1 tablespoon oil
30 g butter
100 g button
  mushrooms, sliced
4 large croissants
1/3 cup cream cheese,
  softened
1 tablespoon finely
  chopped fresh
  basil

1. Preheat oven to moderate 180°C. Trim rind from bacon and cut into short thin strips. Heat oil in a frying pan, cook bacon over medium heat for 5 minutes or until golden. Remove with a slotted spoon; drain.
2. Melt butter in frying pan. Add mushrooms and cook over medium heat for 5 minutes until soft. Remove from pan, discarding any excess liquid.
3. Cut top third from croissants. Hollow out bases slightly; spread each croissant with one quarter of the cream cheese. Spoon cooked bacon and mushrooms onto cheese, replace lid. Place croissants on an oven tray and bake for 10 minutes until heated through. Garnish croissants with finely chopped fresh basil and serve immediately.

# Turkey Muffins

*Preparation time:*
10 minutes
*Total cooking time:*
5 minutes
*Serves 4*

4 English muffins
1 medium avocado,
  mashed
8 slices cooked turkey
  breast
1/2 cup cranberry sauce
125 g brie cheese, sliced
fresh dill sprigs, to
  garnish

1. Preheat grill to moderately hot. Split muffins in half and lightly toast both sides. Spread muffins with avocado, place turkey slices on top.
2. Add a dollop of cranberry sauce to turkey; place a single layer of brie slices over top.
3. Cook under grill for 3–4 minutes until cheese has softened and is starting to melt. Garnish with dill, if desired, and serve at once.

# Salami & Swiss Melt

*Preparation time:*
10 minutes
*Total cooking time:*
5 minutes
*Serves 2–4*

2 flat Turkish breads
50 g butter
8 slices salami
50 g button
  mushrooms
2 teaspoons Italian
  herbs
4 large slices Swiss
  cheese

1. Preheat grill to moderately hot. Cut bread into 4 cm wide pieces; lightly toast outer sides of each half. Spread with butter.
2. Cut salami slices in half and then into short, thin strips; divide between breads. Finely slice mushrooms and arrange over salami slices.
3. Sprinkle with herbs; lay cheese slices on top. Place under grill and cook for 3–4 minutes until cheese is melted and bubbling. Serve immediately.

*From top: Mushroom & Bacon Croissant, Turkey Muffins and Salami & Swiss Melt*

# Chilli Bean Rolls

*Preparation time:*
10 minutes
*Total cooking time:*
13 minutes
*Serves 4*

4 large round brown
  bread rolls
2 teaspoons oil
1 small onion, finely
  chopped
1 small tomato,
  chopped
130 g can corn kernels,
  drained
400 g can Mexican
  chilli beans
2/3 cup grated cheddar
  cheese

1. Preheat oven to
moderate 180°C. Cut a
lid from the top of each
roll; hollow out bread
from inside, leaving a
1.5 cm thick wall.
2. Heat oil in a small
pan. Cook onion over
medium heat for
3 minutes until soft.
Add chopped tomato,
corn and chilli beans
and mix well.
3. Spoon bean mixture
into rolls. Top with
grated cheese, replace
lid of roll. Place on
an oven tray and bake
for 10 minutes until
cheese has melted and
rolls are crisp. Remove
from oven and serve
immediately on
4 serving plates.

# Cheesy Salmon Fingers

*Preparation time:*
15 minutes
*Total cooking time:*
3 minutes
*Serves 2–4*

4 slices thick toast
  bread
210 g can salmon,
  drained
1/4 cup finely grated
  mozzarella cheese
1/4 cup finely grated
  cheddar cheese
1/4 cup tomato pasta
  sauce
2 spring onions, finely
  sliced
1 tablespoon finely
  chopped fresh parsley
fresh oregano sprigs, to
  garnish

1. Preheat grill to
moderately hot. Toast
bread lightly on one
side.
2. Place salmon in
medium mixing bowl
and break up with a
fork. Add cheeses,
sauce, spring onion and
parsley; mix well.
3. Spread salmon
mixture onto untoasted
sides of bread. Remove
crusts from bread and
cut each slice into
3 fingers. Place under

grill and cook for
3 minutes until cheese
is bubbling. Garnish
with oregano sprigs, if
desired, and serve
immediately.

# Chicken, Corn & Avocado Melt

*Preparation time:*
15 minutes
*Total cooking time:*
5 minutes
*Serves 2–4*

4 thick slices corn bread
130 g can creamed corn
8 slices smoked chicken
  breast
1/2 avocado, sliced
2 spring onions, finely
  chopped
3/4 cup grated cheddar
  cheese
paprika

1. Preheat grill to
moderately hot. Toast
bread lightly on both
sides.
2. Spread creamed corn
onto each slice; top
with chicken and
avocado. Sprinkle with
spring onion and
cheese. Dust lightly
with paprika.
3. Place under grill and
cook 2 minutes until
cheese is melted and
bubbling. Serve
immediately.

*From top: Chicken, Corn & Avocado Melt, Cheesy
Salmon Fingers and Chilli Bean Rolls*

# Smoked Salmon Bagels

*Preparation time:*
  5 minutes
*Total cooking time:*
  5 minutes
*Serves 4*

4 bagels
80 g boursin cheese
2 spring onions, finely
  chopped
1 teaspoon finely
  grated lemon rind
1 teaspoon finely
  chopped fresh dill
100 g smoked salmon
  slices

1. Preheat oven to
moderate 180°C.
Cut bagels in half
horizontally and lightly
toast insides.
2. In small mixing bowl
combine cheese, spring
onion, lemon rind and
fresh dill. Spread on
lower half of bagels.
Top with salmon.
3. Replace top of bagel;
place on oven tray.
Bake for 5 minutes,
until bagels are crisp
and heated through.

**Note:** Boursin cheese is
a soft cheese lightly
flavoured with herbs
and garlic. It is found
in most delicatessens
and supermarkets.
Boursin is often served
on a cheese plate.

# Mushrooms en Croute

*Preparation time:*
  15 minutes
*Total cooking time:*
  10 minutes
*Serves 4*

4 large flat mushrooms
1 clove garlic, crushed
40 g butter, melted
1 small avocado, sliced
1 cup grated cheddar
  cheese
1 teaspoon finely
  chopped fresh parsley
4 thick slices white
  bread

1. Preheat oven to
moderate 180°C. Brush
an oven tray with
melted butter or oil.
Remove stems from
mushrooms; wipe with
paper towel or, if
necessary, peel skin
from tops.
2. Place mushrooms
top side down on
prepared tray. Combine
garlic and butter; brush
over mushrooms. Lay
slices of avocado over
mushroom; top with
cheese and parsley.
3. Using a biscuit cutter,
cut rounds from bread
slices. Place on oven
tray with mushrooms.
Bake for 10 minutes,
until cheese has melted
and mushrooms are just
soft. Bread rounds

should be dried out and
slightly golden. Serve
mushrooms on top of
bread rounds.

# Italian Loaf

*Preparation time:*
  15 minutes + 1 hour
  refrigeration
*Total cooking time:*
  15 minutes
*Serves 6*

1 round Italian loaf
¼ cup olive oil
6 slices salami
1 cup marinated
  quartered artichoke
  hearts, drained
½ cup sundried
  tomatoes in oil,
  drained and sliced
1 small red onion,
  finely sliced
¼ cup fresh basil leaves
⅓ cup pitted black
  olives, halved
150 g mozzarella
  cheese, sliced

1. Cut top third from
loaf; hollow out bread
from inside leaving a
2 cm wall. Brush inside
of loaf with oil.
2. Layer salami slices,
artichokes, tomato,
onion, basil, olives and
mozzarella into bread.
Replace lid; wrap bread
tightly in aluminium
foil. Place a small
board with a weight
(such as a can) on top
of loaf.

*From top: Italian Loaf, Smoked Salmon Bagels and Mushrooms en Croute*

**3.** Refrigerate for at least 1 hour to allow flavours to develop. Return to room temperature.
**4.** Preheat oven to moderate 180°C. Bake bread 15 minutes until heated through. Serve.

**Note:** Loaf may be heated through when assembled, but refrigeration will enhance flavour. You may refrigerate bread up to 4 hours before baking.

# Tandoori Chicken

*Preparation time:*
15 minutes +
20 minutes
refrigeration
*Total cooking time:*
20–30 minutes
*Serves 2–4*

1/4 cup natural yoghurt
1 tablespoon tomato
paste
1 tablespoon tandoori
curry blend
2 teaspoons lemon juice
2 chicken breast fillets
2 naan breads, halved
1 small red onion,
finely sliced
1 medium ripe tomato,
cut into thin wedges
1 cup grated cheddar
cheese

**Topping**
6 cos lettuce leaves,
finely shredded
1/4 cup natural yoghurt
2 tablespoons finely
chopped fresh mint
1/2 Lebanese cucumber,
peeled, finely chopped

1. Combine yoghurt,
tomato paste, tandoori
blend and lemon juice
in small bowl. Trim
chicken of excess fat
and sinew; prick
chicken breasts several
times with a fork.
Combine yoghurt
mixture and chicken in
medium bowl. Cover
and refrigerate for
20 minutes.
2. Transfer chicken to
oiled baking dish. Bake
in preheated moderate
180°C oven for
20–30 minutes.
Remove and cool
slightly.
3. **To make topping:**
While chicken is
cooking make topping
by combining lettuce,
yoghurt, mint and
finely chopped
cucumber in a small
serving bowl.
Refrigerate until use.
4. Cut chicken breasts
diagonally into thin
strips. Place naan bread
on foil-lined tray and
top each half with
chicken, red onion,
tomato and cheese.
Place under preheated
grill and cook for
1–2 minutes until
cheese melts. Serve
immediately on a
platter or individual
serving plates
accompanied by
topping which may be
spooned over chicken,
as desired.

**Note:** Tandoori curry
blend may be found on
supermarket shelves. It
will give your curries a
characteristic flavour
and colour.

# Feta Toasts

*Preparation time:*
15 minutes
*Total cooking time:*
5 minutes
*Serves 4*

2 medium tomatoes,
finely chopped
1 small red onion,
finely chopped
2 tablespoons chopped
fresh coriander
1 tablespoon olive oil
2 teaspoons lemon juice
4 thick slices Italian
bread
1/2 cup hummus
100 g feta cheese

1. Combine tomato,
onion, coriander, oil
and juice in a small
bowl; mix well.
2. Lightly toast bread
on both sides. Spread
one side with hummus
and pile tomato
mixture evenly over
hummus.
3. Crumble feta cheese
over tomato, place
under a hot grill for
5 minutes until cheese
is lightly golden. Serve
immediately.

# Toasted Bolognaise

*Preparation time:*
10 minutes
*Total cooking time:*
50 minutes
*Serves 2–4*

1 tablespoon olive oil
1 medium onion, finely
    chopped
2 cloves garlic, crushed
1 tablespoon finely
    chopped fresh parsley
250 g lean beef mince
2 tablespoons tomato
    paste
400 g can tomatoes,
    crushed
1/4 cup white wine
1/4 cup finely chopped
    fresh basil leaves
1/2 teaspoon chilli
    powder
salt and pepper
1 loaf Italian bread, cut
    into thick slices
1/2 cup shaved
    parmesan cheese
fresh parsley sprigs, to
    garnish

1. Heat oil in medium
pan; add finely
chopped onion. Cook
over medium heat for
4 minutes or until
onion is soft. Add
garlic and parsley and
cook for a further
2 minutes.
2. Add mince and cook
for 5 minutes until
browned and almost all
liquid is absorbed.
Break up any lumps
with a fork as it cooks.
Add tomato paste and
cook for a further
2 minutes. Add tomato,
white wine, basil, chilli
powder and salt and
pepper to taste. Bring
to boil, reduce heat to
a simmer and cook a
further 30 minutes or
until sauce thickens and
liquid is reduced.
3. Toast slices of Italian
bread on each side. Top
with bolognaise sauce
and shaved parmesan
cheese. Cook under
preheated grill for
4–5 minutes or until
cheese is melted.
Garnish with parsley
sprigs, if desired, and
serve immediately.

# Spicy Sausage on Corn Bread

*Preparation time:*
25 minutes
*Total cooking time:*
45 minutes
*Serves 2–4*

1 tablespoon olive oil
2 cloves garlic, crushed
1 tablespoon finely
    chopped fresh parsley
4 Italian sausages
1 medium red onion,
    sliced
1/2 green capsicum cut
    into thin strips
1 tablespoon
    tomato paste
400 g can tomatoes,
    crushed
1 tablespoon hot chilli
    sauce
1 tablespoon balsamic
    vinegar
1 tablespoon chopped
    fresh basil
1 teaspoon chopped
    fresh thyme
1 loaf of corn bread
1 cup grated mozzarella
    cheese

1. Heat oil in a non-
stick frying pan, add
crushed garlic and
parsley; cook
over medium heat for
2 minutes. Add
sausages and cook,
turning frequently, until
golden brown. Remove
sausages and set aside.
Add onion and
capsicum and cook for
4 minutes or until
onion is soft. Add
tomato paste and cook,
stirring frequently, for
1 minute. Add tomato,
chilli sauce, vinegar,
basil and thyme. Bring
to boil and reduce heat
to a simmer.
2. Cut the sausages
diagonally into
1 cm slices and return
to the pan; simmer in
sauce a further
25 minutes until sauce
is thickened and liquid
is reduced.
3. Cut corn bread into
2 cm thick slices and
toast on each side.
Top with tomato and
sausage mixture and

*Toasted Bolognaise (top) and Spicy Sausage on Corn Bread*

mozzarella cheese. Grill for a further 2 minutes or until cheese is melted. Serve immediately.

**Note:** Italian sausages come in a variety of flavours, shapes and sizes. For this dish use thin Italian pork sausages. You will find them in the delicatessen section of your supermarket and in most delicatessens.

51

# Chicken Quesadilla (Mexican Melt)

*Preparation time:*
15 minutes
*Total cooking time:*
5 minutes
*Serves 2*

2 flour tortillas
⅓ cup taco sauce
1 cup shredded
   barbecued chicken
1 cup grated cheddar or
   mozzarella cheese
2 spring onions, finely
   chopped
sour cream and
   paprika, to serve

**1.** Heat a dry non-stick frying pan. Place one tortilla in pan and spread lightly with taco sauce. Cook tortilla over medium heat for 2–3 minutes.

**2.** Arrange shredded chicken evenly over tortilla; sprinkle with grated cheese and finely chopped onion. Place second tortilla on top; cook for 2 minutes.
**3.** Turn tortilla over and cook other side until cheese has melted and the quesadilla is heated through. Remove from pan. Cut into wedges. Serve with a small dollop of sour cream sprinkled with paprika, if desired.

**Note:** Tortillas are thin, round flatbreads made from wheat flour or cornmeal.

*Chicken Quesadilla (Mexican Melt)*

*Shred barbecued chicken, grate mozzarella cheese and finely chop spring onions.*

*Place one tortilla in a pan and cover with taco sauce. Cook for 1–2 minutes.*

Top tortilla in pan with chicken, cheese and onion; cover with second tortilla.

Carefully turn tortilla over; slide back into pan and cook on second side.

## Tuna Subs

*Preparation time:*
15 minutes
*Total cooking time:*
10–15 minutes
*Serves 2*

185 g can tuna chunks
  in brine, well drained
6 spring onions, finely
  chopped
1 cup grated cheddar
  cheese
¼ cup sour cream
2 tablespoons
  mayonnaise
1 tablespoon chopped
  fresh parsley
¼ teaspoon sweet
  paprika
2 torpedo rolls
¼ cup thinly
  sliced stuffed olives
  (optional)
½ cup grated cheddar
  cheese, extra

1. Preheat oven to
moderately hot, 210°C
(190°C Gas). Combine
drained tuna, spring
onion, cheese, sour
cream, mayonnaise,
parsley and sweet
paprika in medium
bowl.
2. Make a 1 cm deep
tunnel along the top of
each roll, leaving 1 cm
at each end of roll
intact. Remove half the
doughy centre of each

roll to form a thick
shell. Divide tuna
mixture into two and
fill the centre of each
roll; top with olives, if
desired, and extra
cheese.
3. Place on a foil-lined
oven tray, bake for
10–15 minutes or until
roll is crunchy and
cheese is well melted.
Serve immediately.

## Mozzarella in Carozza

*Preparation time:*
  15 minutes +
  30 minutes standing
*Total cooking time:*
  10 minutes
*Serves 2–4*

45 g can anchovy
  fillets, well drained
4 slices mozzarella
  cheese, 1 cm thick
1 large ripe tomato,
  sliced
8 thick slices white
  bread, crusts removed
1–2 teaspoons dried
  oregano leaves
salt and pepper
3 eggs, lightly beaten
oil for shallow frying
fresh basil sprigs
halved cherry tomatoes,
  to garnish

1. Halve each anchovy
fillet with a knife. Cut

each slice of mozzarella
in half. Cut tomato
slices in half. Halve
bread slices lengthways.
Top 8 slices of bread
with mozzarella,
anchovies and tomato;
sprinkle with oregano,
salt and pepper. Cover
with remaining 8 bread
slices to make 8 small
oblong sandwiches.
2. Place beaten eggs in
large rectangular
shallow dish. Dip
sandwiches in the egg
and press down so that
the bread soaks up egg.
Leave to soak for
30 minutes turning
sandwiches carefully
every 10 minutes.
3. Heat oil in frying
pan to moderately hot
and carefully fry the
sandwiches for
2–3 minutes on each
side, or until golden
brown. Remove with
tongs or a slotted
spoon; drain on paper
towels. Serve hot,
garnished with fresh
basil sprigs and cherry
tomatoes, if desired.

*Mozzarella in Carozza (top)
and Tuna Subs*

55

# Crab Triangles

*Preparation time:*
15 minutes
*Total cooking time:*
5 minutes
*Serves 4*

1 cm piece lemon grass,
  chopped
1 clove garlic, chopped
2 spring onions,
  chopped
1 cm piece fresh ginger
1 teaspoon ground
  coriander
200 g can crabmeat,
  well drained
100 g ricotta cheese
8 slices white bread
fresh parsley sprigs, to
  garnish

1. Place lemon grass, garlic, spring onions, ginger and coriander in a food processor bowl; process 30 seconds or until mixture is almost a paste. Transfer to medium mixing bowl and combine with crabmeat and ricotta.
2. Toast bread under preheated grill on one side until golden. Turn bread over and spread each slice with 1 tablespoon of crabmeat mixture on untoasted side.
3. Return to grill for 2–3 minutes. Halve diagonally. Serve, garnished with fresh parsley.

# Crostini

*Preparation time:*
15 minutes
*Total cooking time:*
8 minutes
*Serves 4*

1 small French bread
  stick (about 30 cm
  long)
¼ cup olive oil
1 clove garlic, crushed
1 tablespoon tomato
  paste
1 tablespoon mashed
  anchovies
100 g bocconcini
  cheese, thinly sliced
fresh basil leaves, to
  serve

1. Preheat oven to moderate 180°C. Cut bread into 1.5 cm slices. Place in a single layer on an oven tray and cook for 5 minutes, until just crisp and dry.
2. Combine oil and garlic and brush onto bread slices. Spread lightly with combined tomato paste and anchovies; top with bocconcini.
3. Return slices to oven for 3 minutes until cheese has melted. Garnish each slice with basil leaf, if desired.

**Note:** Bocconcini is fresh mozzarella and comes in small round balls stored in liquid.

# Mushroom Bites

*Preparation time:*
20 minutes
*Total cooking time:*
30 minutes
*Serves 4*

30 g butter
4 spring onions, finely
  chopped
250 g button
  mushrooms, finely
  diced
½ teaspoon green
  peppercorns
½ teaspoon ground
  coriander
½ teaspoon ground
  cumin
½ teaspoon sweet
  paprika
1 tablespoon
  wholegrain mustard
2 tablespoons sweet
  sherry
½ cup thick cream
salt and pepper
1 baguette loaf
¼ cup finely chopped
  fresh parsley
½ cup shaved parmesan
  cheese

1. Heat butter in a frying pan, add spring onions; cook over medium heat for 2 minutes or until soft. Add mushrooms, peppercorns, coriander, cumin and paprika and cook for a further 8 minutes. Stir in mustard and sherry; reduce heat. Cook for

*From top: Mushroom Bites, Crab Triangles and Crostini*

2 minutes. Add cream. Simmer over low heat for 8–10 minutes or until sauce thickens and is reduced. Remove from heat and allow to cool slightly.
2. Cut baguette loaf diagonally into 1 cm slices. Toast lightly under preheated grill on each side until golden brown. Top each slice with 2–3 teaspoons of mushroom mixture, sprinkle lightly with parsley and top with shaved parmesan.
3. Return to grill and cook for 2 minutes or until parmesan is almost melted. Serve immediately.

# Huevos Rancheros

*Preparation time:*
20 minutes
*Total cooking time:*
20 minutes
*Serves 2*

2 tablespoons olive oil
1 medium red onion,
    sliced
1 small green capsicum,
    finely sliced
2 cloves garlic, crushed
1 tablespoon finely
    chopped fresh
    continental parsley
440 g can tomatoes,
    crushed
½ teaspoon chilli
    powder
2 eggs
2 x 20 cm soft flour
    tortillas
salt and freshly ground
    black pepper
1 cup grated cheddar
    cheese
45 g can anchovy
    fillets, drained
1 tablespoon chopped
    capers

1. Heat oil in medium frying pan. Add onion and capsicum and cook over low heat for 4–5 minutes or until soft. Add garlic and parsley and cook for 2 minutes. Add tomato and chilli, bring to boil. Reduce heat and simmer for 6 minutes.
2. Using a spoon, make two holes in tomato mixture. Break one egg into each hole. Cook until eggs are set.
3. Place tortillas on a foil-lined grill tray. Using an egg slice, place half the tomato mixture and one egg on each tortilla. Sprinkle with salt, pepper and grated cheese. Decorate with finely sliced anchovy fillets and capers. Cook under preheated grill for 2 minutes or until cheese has melted.

# Smoked Trout & Horseradish

*Preparation time:*
15 minutes
*Total cooking time:*
5 minutes
*Serves 2–4*

100 g cream cheese
1–2 tablespoons
    horseradish cream
2 tablespoons sour
    cream
2 crusty Italian-style
    rolls
340 g can asparagus
    spears, drained
100 g packet smoked
    ocean trout
sliced small lemon
    wedges, to garnish

1. Beat cream cheese, horseradish cream and sour cream in medium bowl until smooth. Cut the rolls in half horizontally and place on a grill tray. Toast rolls on both sides under preheated grill.
2. Remove from grill and spread the cut face of each roll with 2–3 tablespoons of the cheese and horseradish mixture. Heat under grill until horseradish mixture is warm. Top with asparagus spears (if the spears are thick cut them in half lengthways) and sliced ocean trout.
3. Garnish with the lemon wedges, if desired, and serve immediately.

**Note:** Fresh asparagus can be used instead of tinned, if preferred. Prepare fresh asparagus by trimming the stalks and plunging them in boiling water for 2 minutes or until just tender. Drain at once. Cut spears in half lengthways if they are very thick.

*Huevos Rancheros (top) and Smoked Trout &*
*Horseradish*

# Veal Parmigiana Melt

*Preparation time:*
20 minutes
*Total cooking time:*
20 minutes
*Serves 2–4*

200 g *thinly sliced veal*
1 *egg, lightly beaten*
2 *cups fresh or dried breadcrumbs*
*oil for shallow frying*
1 *Vienna loaf*
½ *quantity pizza sauce (page 5)*
120 g *mozzarella cheese, sliced*
*freshly ground black pepper, to serve*

**1.** Trim veal of excess fat and sinew. Dip veal into egg mixture and coat with breadcrumbs. Place on tray, cover and refrigerate for about 10 minutes.
**2.** Heat oil in medium frying pan until moderately hot. Cook a few veal slices in pan for 2–3 minutes on each side or until golden brown. Remove from heat and drain on paper towels. Repeat with remaining veal.
**3.** Cut Vienna loaf in thick diagonal slices. Lightly toast bread slices on each side. Spread with butter, if desired. Top each bread slice with one portion of cooked veal, 2 tablespoons of pizza sauce and a slice of mozzarella. Place under a preheated grill and cook for 3–4 minutes until sauce is warmed and cheese is melted. Sprinkle with freshly ground black pepper, if desired. Serve immediately.

# Ham & Eggs Benedict with Cheese

*Preparation time:*
10 minutes
*Total cooking time:*
5 minutes
*Serves 2*

4 *eggs*
2 *tablespoons milk*
1 *tablespoon chopped fresh chives*
30 g *butter*
2 *wholemeal English muffins*
30 g *butter, extra*
2 *slices smoked ham, chopped*
½ *cup grated cheddar cheese*
*fresh thyme sprigs, to garnish*

**1.** Place eggs, milk and chives in medium mixing bowl and whisk until combined. Melt butter in medium pan and pour in egg mixture; stir gently over low heat for 2–3 minutes until eggs are set but still creamy. Remove from heat and set aside.
**2.** Split muffins in half horizontally. Lightly toast muffins for 1–2 minutes on each side. Spread with extra butter. Top each muffin with smoked ham, scrambled egg and grated cheese. Place under preheated grill and cook 1–2 minutes or until cheese has melted. Garnish with thyme, if desired, and serve immediately.

**Note:** Smoked ham can be replaced with prosciutto, salami, smoked salmon or trout. Fresh hollandaise sauce may be served as a variation. Delete cheese if using sauce.

*Ham & Eggs Benedict with Cheese (top) and Veal Parmigiana Melt*

# Fruity Chocolate Melt

*Preparation time:*
  15 minutes
*Cooking time:*
  5 minutes
*Serves 2*

*4 thick slices fruit loaf*
*½ cup ricotta cheese*
*2 large bananas, sliced*
  *diagonally*
*30 g dark chocolate,*
  *grated*
*ice cream, to serve*

**1.** Preheat grill to moderately hot. Toast bread lightly on both sides.
**2.** Spread toast with cheese and top with banana slices. Sprinkle grated chocolate over banana.
**3.** Place toast under preheated grill and cook until chocolate has melted and banana is warmed through. Serve at once with scoop of ice cream, if desired.

**Note:** Ricotta cheese is fresh Italian cheese which is soft and smooth textured. It is mild flavoured and used in both savoury and sweet dishes.

# Apricot Brioche Melt

*Preparation time:*
  10 minutes
*Cooking time:*
  1–2 minutes
*Serves 2–4*

*4 thick slices brioche*
*150 g cream cheese*
*⅓ cup chopped dried*
  *apricots*
*1 tablespoon chopped*
  *glacé ginger*
*2 tablespoons flaked*
  *almonds*

**1.** Toast brioche slices lightly on both sides.
**2.** Place cheese, chopped apricots and ginger in a small bowl and mix until well combined. Spread onto toasted brioche and top with flaked almonds.
**3.** Place under preheated grill for 30–40 seconds until the cheese has softened and almonds are golden. Serve immediately.

*Apricot Brioche Melt (top)*
*and Fruity Chocolate Melt*

# Index